THEM=US

Tibor Kalman

LIZ FARRELLY

tibor kalman
design and
undesign

First published in 1998 in the United States of America by
Watson-Guptill Publications, a division of
Billboard Publications, Inc.,
1515 Broadway, New York, NY 10036

Library of Congress CIP data applied for.

ISBN 0-8230-1146-1

This book was conceived, designed, and produced by
THE IVY PRESS LTD
2/3 St Andrew's Place
Lewes, East Sussex BN7 1UP

Art director: TERRY JEAVONS
Design and page layout: ALAN OSBAHR
Commissioning editor: CHRISTINE DAVIS
Managing editor: ANNE TOWNLEY

Printed in Hong Kong

Contents

"**W**hy? Because I am lucky. Lucky to have been born in 1949. I got to live in and remember a real live Communist country until I was seven. I got to escape in the middle of the night. I got to live in 1950s suburban America. I got to be a caddie and to make burgers at a fast food restaurant. I got to college in 1968. What luck! I got to participate in the radical student movement, witness the birth of feminism (I think it was on a Friday), hear Janis Joplin and Jimi Hendrix and Roland Kirk and Vladimir Horowitz, and still managed to cut sugarcane in Cuba. I was around (and skinny and in my twenties!) for the sexual revolution of the 70s. I started a design company (and made money!) in the 80s. I got to spec type and do mechanicals and understand how things get *made*. Now I'm getting to participate in the explosion of information and media in the 90s, and now I'm finally beginning to understand the power of communications and have the opportunity to create content and direction for my work. Plus, I married a beautiful, smart, funny woman and have two wonderful and funny kids (one of each!). Wow! Let's do it again. Only this time, let's make it exactly the same (except for the bell-bottoms)."

Tibor Kalman

TIBOR KALMAN INHABITS a unique position within the realm of visual culture, so much so that to categorize him as a graphic designer would be to miss the point by a mile. The title of editor, filmmaker or product designer could all equally apply. To describe his career as diverse is also to err on the side of understatement. His far-from-run-of-the-mill projects include editing *Colors*, arguably the most controversial youth-oriented magazine ever to hit the world's streets; writing planning guidelines for the redevelopment of New York's notorious 42nd Street; launching and selling a range of must-have products; art directing pop innovators Talking Heads, on video and in print; and co-curating and designing the critically acclaimed New York art survey, *City of Ambition*, at the Whitney Museum of American Art.

One of Kalman's great achievements has been to break down the barriers between the different design media and disciplines, leaving the way open for others to venture out of their specializations. He puts his thirst for experimentation down to "a short attention span. I get really bored really easily so I like to do no more than two projects of any single type. The third will already be a bore, or it'll come out boring, even worse."

Ask him his opinion of graphic design and he'll reply with an irreverent quip, "it's not brain surgery." That's typical Kalman wit, brutally honest, no messing. Expanding beyond the tightly defined area of design, he has also ventured beyond the close-knit community where he first made his mark, the New York graphics

"Many designers believe that design is the end product. To me, design is merely a language, a means to an end, a means of communication. The question is, what do you communicate— Burger King, or something meaningful?"

Colors challenged racial stereotypes by transforming well-known personalities. Unsurprisingly, the tabloid press revealed their own true colors.

8

scene, to become an outspoken figure on a wider stage. Backing up his claim to love controversy, he can produce several volumes of press-clippings culled from the world's media. That notoriety reached new heights during his days at *Colors*, when the tabloid press discovered Kalman.

Able to give as good as he gets, as a hard-line commentator Kalman revels in debunking the self-importance and overindulgence that he believes is rife within design and publishing. Spiced with a note of self-deprecation and a generous sprinkling of irreverence, Kalman's writings and lectures challenge designers to face up to the consequences of their actions, and choose between simply greasing the wheels of commerce or making a very real contribution to change.

"A designer is a professional liar because he's hired not to make the properties of a product clear but to enhance the product beyond its truth. In a funny sort of way it's exactly what lawyers do with the moral position of a company, and what accountants do with the figures. Still, graphic designers think they're doing something else, making beautiful art, but it's just not true." Kalman's antidote to corporate compromise is work for what he calls his own "private audience." "The sense in which we were our own audience was that we'd look at a project and say, never mind the client, do we think this is cool?" His attitude may sound self-indulgent, but behind the bluff is a logic that facilitates honesty. Put simply, it's very hard to lie to yourself.

Coming from the outside

How is it that Kalman has assumed the role of spokesperson, and is so critical of the petty concerns of designer stylists? Coming from "Budapest via upstate New York" instilled Kalman with attitude. "I've always considered myself an outsider and I've always tried to do good by being bad. It might be a contrarian attitude, but it's what I believe works."

An education peppered with journalism, informed by the radical politics of the late 1960s, fine-tuned Kalman's conscience. Spotting an opportunity to "get out of the basement, where I was alphabetizing books" (at Barnes & Noble, the New York book store), he worked on a window display one weekend. His enthusiasm for not alphabetizing books led him to suggest more displays and signage. He admits that "it was kind of obnoxious and audacious," but he went on to head up an in-house design department for 11 years, establishing a visual identity for a world-renowned brand. (Barnes & Noble has grown into a chain with hundreds of outlets.)

With no formal design training, Kalman was able to find his own aesthetic. But it was no overnight success story. He describes his work for Barnes & Noble as "better than the displays at Woolworth's. I was rudely self-taught, and it was a few years into running M&Co [which Kalman and partners Carol Bokuniewicz and Liz Trorato set up in 1979] before the work was even remotely reasonable."

M&Co was staffed with the brightest graduates from New York's avant-garde design colleges, including Stephen Doyle, Alex

TALKINGHEADS

A logo for Talking Heads turns typography on its head but retains legibility.

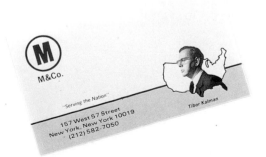

Tibor Kalman's calling card parodies that of an insurance or car salesman of 1950s industrial America.

Isley, Emily Oberman, and Stefan Sagmeister—all of whom have subsequently made their mark as individuals on New York's design scene. Kalman instigated an intense regime for generating ideas, encouraging designers to "let their hands draw" and to rely on their unconscious. "If you sink into your consciousness enough you'll come up with something fresh and clean. We'd end up with a room full of crumpled yellow paper if it was a good session."

There was another important, if uncredited, player in the company. "It used to be a secret that the 'M' in M&Co was dedicated to Maira, my collaborator, lover, and wife," says Kalman. "We've been together since we were 18 and are really good friends, and I'm pretty invested in her as a critic. It wasn't just me—everyone at M&Co would go to Maira for her weird, off the wall, lateral ideas, as opposed to the logical ideas we'd come up with."

Kalman's survival tactic was attack. He would pursue clients with whom he was keen to work. When the possibility arose of working with David Byrne he assured the nascent star that he was "born to do the project." Working on spec, M&Co pitched "two billion ideas" for their first Talking Heads album cover design. Other tactics were employed to stave off boredom. "I was willing to mess up the process. Just because a client said they wanted a brochure, that didn't necessarily mean they needed a brochure. I always considered my clients' clients to be the audience. This enabled me to considerably broaden the spectrum of projects we worked on. When you're working in an area you're unfamiliar with, it's the best thing there is; you feel like a ten-year-old boy, not knowing what you're doing and in awe of the possibilities—everything is possible, and nothing is impossible. It is the greatest state a designer could be in."

At M&Co Kalman took on the role of creative director. The company's young designers were treated as collaborators, and clients became friends. "I would use the advice of the people who were around, especially Maira," Kalman recalls, but since he is a self-confessed dictator (he once called himself an "Aesthetic Overlord" on *Interview's* masthead) nothing left the studio without Kalman first being convinced of its worth.

This distilling process led to design. solutions that presented complex ideas in the most transparent of visual languages, across a wide spread of media and aimed at a multitude of audiences. "We were constantly scared to death that David Byrne would discover our bank brochures and our bank clients would find out we were doing record covers. It was almost like playing Robin Hood. We took money from the rich clients and spent it on the poor clients. The rich clients were banks, real estate, and suchlike, and the poor clients were rock bands, museums, and so on. In fact, the first time we showed a potential client our 'hip' and 'straight' work together was five years after we had done our first Talking Heads cover. Thinking logically I, as a client, would be excited that a designer could do it both ways. But clients really started getting hipper (and younger) only after the mid-80s."

With M&Co's "$26 Cash for Christmas," the recipient had to decide whether to use the pre-addressed charity envelopes, or pocket the cash.

The new buzz enabled M&Co to move between what many believed to be mutually exclusive areas of interest. Kalman had recognized that the corporate work was changing and that baby-boomers in suits were now running the banks. He tapped into a new generation of professionals who were receptive to pop culture. It was a case of right time, right face. And while producing communications solutions for powerful corporate clients, Kalman was also operating within the city's low-budget cultural arenas. In New York, the division wasn't simply aesthetic, it was a cultural and economic chasm that few crossed. Only now, the businesspeople were looking for a make-over.

M&Co adopted another up-front strategy to feed the buzz. Every Christmas Kalman and his designers would dream up and mail out a gift. "It was the one project a year when we could throw our creative weight around without interference from a client, because we were the client. Sometimes it succeeded and sometimes it screwed up. We'd send something to people we had no business talking to, like a sales call, show our friends how cool we were, and teach our clients the lesson that if they left us alone this was what we could do." One gift contained a thought-provoking text along with an amount of cash, and posed fundamental questions about the whole notion of seasonal giving and receiving in relation to actual need. "It was meant to be a very manipulative little present, a conscience bomb." Suffice to say some people found M&Co's Christmas gifts a little too ethically challenging.

The logo for John Sayles' film was painstakingly made to resemble amateur typography.

MATEWAN

"It was almost like playing Robin Hood. We took money from the rich clients and spent it on the poor clients."

In the Chiat Day video, the audience is forced to "close the gaps" and make their own connections.

Non-design and anti-design

Kalman may be a man with a mission, but, thankfully, his preferred tactics save him from falling into the trap of dogma. In an attempt to make design more friendly, and put back the mark of the "human hand," Kalman aims to eradicate what he calls "off-the-shelf graphic design aromas." At M&Co, he says, they "took away all decoration and style." Drawn to unschooled, vernacular advertising and signage, with its honest fallibility and studied effort, Kalman's aesthetic was mutating into a form of non-design, a playful rejection of high-brow theory and tasteful elitism.

"Our first real attempt at a vernacular logo was for *Matewan*, a film by John Sayles. We messed up the type and spacing to make it look like someone had tried to do it really nicely, with a lot of time and very little skill," recalls Kalman. "I consciously distanced myself from the graphics world once I started on the notion that ugliness was more interesting than beauty... that stuff which is human, interesting, fucked up, passionate rather than logical, reasonable and, of course, beautiful."

Combining a generous helping of humor, alongside absurd juxtaposition and a celebration of found type and image, Kalman creates visual and verbal messages that oscillate between the familiar and the vague. He mixes unpretentious hooks with unresolved elements, leaving it up to the audience to complete the message. Kalman used this device for a promotional presentation for advertising agency Chiat Day. Images and text slide among three video screens on which a ten-year-old boy, standing in a field next to the Pacific Ocean (overprinted with the word "religion"), explains the agency's philosophy. The screens change to close-ups of a mixing bowl accompanied by the cook's voiceover discussing how the agency works, just as if she were reciting a recipe, while the instructions for making tiramisu appear on screen. Finally, Kalman takes over to demonstrate the differences between "beeg" and "leetle" clients, with the aid of two different-sized fish in a goldfish bowl.

"It was very challenging for the audience," says Kalman. "It was intended to find clients who responded to creativity rather than just cost. Because it's up to you to close the circle, you become a participant in the process, and the information stays with you much longer. It's a technique I use a lot in my lectures as well. Just put discordant pieces up [on the screen] and let people make the connections. Now that runs contrary to communications design but sometimes if you make things clear, it's not as penetrating as if you leave gaps. The trick is to make sure the gaps are spannable."

At the 1986 American Institute of Graphic Art (AIGA) conference, which Kalman co-chaired with Milton Glaser, he recalls the graphic design community's hostility toward his way of thinking. "There was our gang (Neville Brody, Karrie Jacobs, Rick Vermuelen, Gerard Hadders, and others), and we were the people dressed in black, and there were all the other sweet folk, dressed in designer colors, saying, 'they're trying to destroy the business of graphic design.' And maybe we were."

Kalman makes his audience work by pushing the limits of legibility, whether in a spread for Interview *or a call for entries for the AIGA.*

athol fugard gives the impression that doing the right thing is easy, that doing the right thing makes you feel alive, that it is as easy as breathing to know the right way from the wrong way.

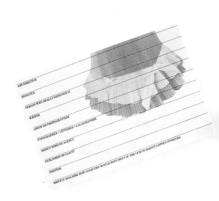

New directions

Looking for a new challenge, and a way of distancing himself from the narrower confines of design, Kalman phased himself into the world of magazines. As art director of *Artforum,* and later as creative director of *Interview,* he worked alongside editor Ingrid Sischy, whom he thanks as "the person who taught me how to look at pictures." Kalman enjoyed complete artistic freedom to design each layout as a visual interpretation of the article. With *Interview,* the effect was blunter: "I was essentially making [layouts like] posters. Since it was a personality magazine, for the opening spread you could just get away with adding the name to a photo."

Kalman soon came to realize that "you either control content or style." He had come to consider design as styling and content to be supreme. In the fall of 1990 the offer came to control both, on a new magazine sponsored by the Benetton company. Kalman assumed a new role, as editor-in-chief of *Colors,* a concept waiting to be invented.

"The whole idea of *Colors* was to make something that was universal." Printing bilingual issues in a range of languages teamed with English, with up to half a million copies distributed worldwide, the aim was to show "the ways in which people around the globe are alike and the ways in which they're different." That involved asking "goofy" questions, briefing researchers to collect the minutiae of everyday living from Helsinki to Guatemala City. By focusing on details (breakfast, hair, snacks), the aim was to create empathy while highlighting cultural, social, spiritual, and economic differences.

Design-wise the idea was to present information with a zero degree of design—as clearly and as concisely as possible. The editorial process, in a term borrowed from Marxist criticism, was one of "successive approximation." This meant that at every stage, including concept, research, writing and layout, "we would keep rethinking the story from the beginning and try to figure out what it should be about."

The ultimate example of this approach was Kalman's last issue of *Colors* (number 13, September 1995). It comprises a journey through the physical world from the macro to the micro (an idea borrowed from Ray and Charles Eames' short film, *Powers of Ten*). The story is told through picture selection and juxtaposition. The issue is totally wordless. Kalman had evolved a design language that functioned on a global level, by allowing a culturally diverse readership to contemplate both the particular and the universal concept. "*Colors* is about not designing anything—it's what I call contemporary anthropology."

At the end of 1995 Kalman left Rome and *Colors* to return to New York, still looking to instigate his own project. "I'm awed by the possibilities of biology and nature; by the potential of the human brain; by architecture, planning, film, and type, even business. I can't believe how much there is to investigate, to learn, and to explore. I want to spend the rest of my life doing that."

"One of the ideas behind *Colors* was to present information with a zero degree of design."

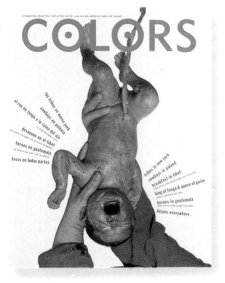

A magazine is born, and the cover of the first issue pulls no punches.

13

Graphics

FROM LOGOS FOR CLOTHING companies (Carbonell and Isaac Mizrahi) to promotional material for the American Institute of Graphic Arts (AIGA); from advertising to restaurant identities, Kalman has worked on an enormous range of graphic projects for an extremely diverse clientele.

"The vernacular approach came in the early 1980s when I became bored with making stuff look 'pretty.' The thing I like about vernacular is that it's real. I don't like graphic design when it is processed through such a bunch of filters that there's no passion left in it, or no 'human hand' left, whereas vernacular design is just that. The early Barnes & Noble work was vernacular because I didn't know any better. I was using horrendous colors—mustards and browns—and I did a rubdown letterhead in Omnibus, the world's second ugliest typeface (after University Roman). But it was still more elegant than the vernacular I like.

"Designing can become very formulaic, so after our third annual report I said 'never again.' M&Co design was about having the idea, and when we eventually figured that out, in the mid-1980s, we took away all the decoration and style. We would try to strip style away.

"Restaurant Florent was a lovely collaboration between M&Co and the owner, Florent Morellet. We developed a whole bunch of new ideas there. And it began with the simplest postcard image. It was actually Florent himself who started the ball rolling. He bought a downtrodden diner, the R&L Luncheonette, in the most difficult street to find in Manhattan. And what he decided to do, in that brilliant Parisian way, was to leave it alone. He wanted the original clientele to stay, the truck drivers and meat packers, but they gradually drifted off as the trendies took over.

"Florent had no money, so when we met he was already into the vernacular. We decided to leave the original name up and just put the

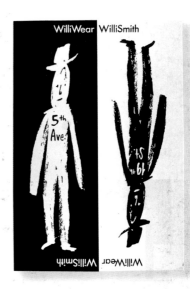

WILLIWEAR/
WILLISMITH
Poster, 1988

A poster announces a new location for the WilliWear store, at the intersection of 19th Street and 5th Avenue.

RESTAURANT
FLORENT
Postcards, 1986

Clip art, a relabeled anatomical drawing, and the cheapest stock are combined to produce an infinitely flexible identity, taking something naive and enlivening it with a hint of absurdist irony.

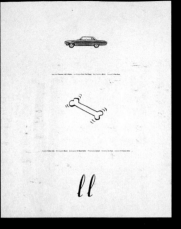

CARBONELL
Press ad, 1988

An advertisement for a Manhattan fashion designer/retailer uses a series of naive illustrations to spell out the company name.

AIGA HUMOR SHOW
Call for entries, 1986

A mocked-up mishap, complete with banana skin, debunks the prestigious American Institute of Graphic Arts. The instruction to the printer—"watch the trimming on this job, it's for the AIGA!"—is embarrassingly revealed as the trim is hopelessly imprecise.

RESTAURANT FLORENT
Matchbooks, 1987

Matchbooks in reverse, with the fancy craft paper on the inside and the address hidden by the matches.

RESTAURANT FLORENT
Press ad, 1988

Stock photography is another of the Restaurant Florent identity-ingredients, and the cheaper the better. A combination of sketchy pictograms and agrotechnology from the 1950s maps the route from field to plate made by a juicy steak. The result is brutally honest and even a touch surreal.

69 Gansevoort Street → Open 24 hours → 989-5779

Restaurant Florent

FUCK BUSH. VOTE.

RESTAURANT FLORENT
Press ad, 1988

Kalman and Florent declared their political preferences during the 1988 presidential campaign. The no-nonsense capitalized type squeezes any opposition off the page.

15

world's simplest neon sign, "Florent," in the window, which cost $100. The matchbooks came first, then we put ads in the early issues of *Paper* magazine, trading on the location being the meat market with a picture of a steak—but no address or telephone. That created a buzz, so Florent then wanted postcards he could hand out in the restaurant and through a mailing list. The first card had six symbols. Alex Isley came up with the whole concept and brought it to me when it was finished, but I had another idea for a symbol, the gun, for New York. All the images came from the *Yellow Pages*.

"For the menu we used old, kind of stupid typefaces (which we considered vernacular and other people considered nostalgic) with fuzzy, black and white images from stock photography agencies. We used all those things because they were all we could afford. What's the stupidest way to advertise a restaurant? An ad with a salt shaker. And when Florent started opening for breakfast, Neil Selkirk took a photograph of a cup, a water glass and a wine glass, which stood for the three meals in the day. When the restaurant went 24 hours, Tim Horn made a card with a hole in it, blue on one side and yellow on the other, representing the moon and the sun.

"Ambiguity is a popular design solution. It's appeal is based on the idea that if you don't get it, it must be cool. What bullshit! All the same, we weren't innocent of that. We did an ad that was a photograph of a field of cows and put 'Fish Specials' on it to say, we serve fish as well. It was ambiguous but with a very specific intention—the audience was meant to get it.

"There was no single look for Florent, and as the owner had a great sense of humor he let us include jokes on the menu (but stopped us short of inventing dishes). During the 1988 presidential campaign we produced the anti-Bush ad and the "potato head" ad picturing Dan Quayle—a reference to the Vice-President's famous mis-

spelling of "potato" on a school visit. Lo and behold, the restaurant took off and became the coolest place in town.

"For fashion designer Isaac Mizrahi, who is a friend, we did a logo and eventually some ads for *W, Vogue,* and *Women's Wear.* Isaac was trying to develop a different kind of informal, experiential approach to fashion, showing that fashion is a process, not just an end result photographed against a white, seamless backdrop. The photo is by the great English photographer Nick Wapplington.

"The Rights of Man poster was designed for the 200th anniversary of the 1789 Proclamation of the Rights of Man. The French design group Grapus gave a whole bunch of designers an Article to illustrate and make into a poster. The results were exhibited all over France. Ours was 'Equality among men' and the text of the Article is simply printed over the face."

ISAAC MIZRAHI
Press ad, 1991

This documentary-style shoot, by British photographer Nick Wapplington, captures the back-stage creative process of fashion design.

Article 35

Quand le gouvernement viole les

droits du peuple

l'insurrection est pour le peuple,

et pour chaque portion du peuple,

le plus sacré des droits

et le plus indispensable

des devoirs.

Images Internationales pour les Droits de l'Homme et du Citoyen

ARTIS 89

THE RIGHTS
OF MAN
Poster, 1989

**This contribution to
an exhibition about the
French Proclamation of the
Rights of Man illustrates
"Equality." The full text
of the Article is printed
over the face of a black
woman, suggesting
that the words are
being spoken.**

KALMAN HAS ART DIRECTED exhibition catalogs, photography monographs, and commercial brochures. He also collaborates with his wife Maira, who writes and illustrates children's books.

"*Strange Attractors: Signs of Chaos* was an exhibition at the New Museum, a small private museum down on Broadway. The curators chose artists who would interpret the word 'chaos' in different ways. There were a lot of Mandelbrot fractals, and M&Co designed the installation and catalog. They didn't have a nickel, so up and down the walls and all over the ceilings we pasted black and white 'public domain' images—cheap Xeroxes of car crashes, train accidents, earthquakes, fires, and disasters. The art was hung right on top of that chaotic space because the idea was, why shouldn't art have to compete with the real world, why should it be seen in a white box?

"We gave the curators a very simple challenge and they rose to it. We said, since you're doing a show about chaos, can we make an exhibition design and catalog which does essentially what a piece of art does, that asks questions and contributes to the visual study of chaos? They said, 'sure.' The catalog is sold in the open position and there's one piece of paper which holds the whole thing together, so you have to break the seal, a tear-off strip, which was also the exhibition brochure. That focuses you in the middle of the book, but there is a definite front and back cover as well. The book is spiral-bound so you can turn it round.

"I worked on the project with Marleen McCarthy. We took each text, the interviews and essays, and put them in different styles (we used the same typeface throughout, though, because I thought that would have been too easy). We created variations in the settings, so a story would start out with one kind of word spacing and leading, and end up with a whole different kind, and some text would be set in fractal shapes. We also wrote some computer programs which changed the weight and capitalization, or italicized the type. So we ended up randomizing it. Of course it never turns out the way you expect, which is the whole point.

"The Swiss furniture manufacturer Vitra is an incredibly interesting company and Rolf Fehlbaum, the chief executive, must be the most sophisticated client I've ever had. The challenge was to make furniture catalogs which would be more editorially oriented, and that would be language-free to avoid the boredom of translation since the catalogs go all over the world. We came up with *Workspirit*, which is a cross between a magazine, a catalog, an annual report, and an update of new products and ideas. It comes out every two years.

"All the images of the furniture were shot, but lots of the other pictures came from stuff I had seen come across my desk at *Colors*. Part of the reason was that at that point my obsession with the vernacular had broadened into an obsession with what used to be called the Third World, and I was trying to figure out how it is that the things that happen in the developing

STRANGE
ATTRACTORS:
SIGNS OF
CHAOS
Exhibition catalog, 1989

Matching the chaos of both the featured artworks and his own installation design, Kalman employed a myriad disruptive devices to make reading this catalog a chaotic act in itself. The back cover *(right)* **features Mandelbrot's own text.**

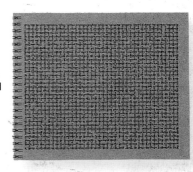

Dan Reynolds. Untitled. 1989. Collection Prudential Insurance Company, New York

technologies.
y have been
en the once
ems to have
– the "phase
endence"; of
f the decay,
rmation. It
essay in the
he strangely

debook, The
in 1983. In
he first exhi-
cientists and
as art.[2] By
as of fractal
of practicing

STRANGE
ATTRACTORS
SIGNS OF
CHAOS

WORKSPIRIT
Catalog for Vitra, 1994

While working on *Colors* Kalman was asked to produce a publication for the office furniture manufacturer Vitra, and took the opportunity to broaden their customers' horizons. Commissioned images are mixed with documentary photography to draw formal comparisons and create striking contrasts. The message is conveyed via subtle resonance.

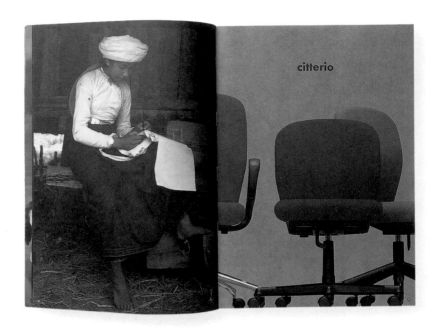

countries are better than those in the industrial-ized countries. I'm interested in investigating the ways in which people with no money, and no industrial culture, do things that are smarter than people who have money and history and computers available to them. That's a big subject to me, and *Colors* and *Workspirit* were about that.

"At the beginning, images of the products smoothly interact with the other images. We would find a form within the product that matched one in the non-industrial image. There were three reasons for this. One, no language; two, developing countries are less familiar; and three, it's kind of embarrassing to do a catalog for very expensive office furniture with all the things that are going on in the world, all the problems. So *Workspirit* is meant to remind you that there is a real world out there, that office furniture is not everything.

"But there's a fine line between those images being respectful and exploitative. And you try to figure out why some images look wrong, and some look proud. The thing is, you don't know what you're doing when you're out there on the edge. You make mistakes all the time, and it takes a while to figure it out. I think the second edi-tion of *Workspirit*, which I worked on with the writer Michael Rock, was in some ways better, but in other ways it didn't have the same energy. We were more careful.

"My collaborations with Jenny Holzer have been wonderful, and continue to this day. There is a famous Sunday supplement in Germany called *Süddeutsche Zeitung*, and every year they turn over an issue to an artist. They gave it to Jenny, and she called me in because the medium was a magazine—and then we did a project which had nothing to do with magazines. She had written texts about rape, and I suggested that we handwrite them in ball-point pen onto women's bodies, so that they would be like tat-toos or markings. She liked the idea, and we just photographed them and laid them out full-bleed.

"On the cover of the magazine was a card which is printed, partially, in human blood. Can you imagine what the publishers said when we

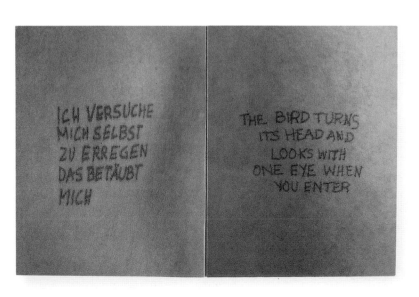

SÜDDEUTSCHE ZEITUNG, NO.46
Magazine spreads, collaboration with Jenny Holzer, 1993

The idea to write artist Jenny Holzer's disturbing texts directly onto female flesh, in an approximation of amateur tattoos, came from Kalman. With the photographs laid out full-bleed, the viewer cannot avoid the message. This controversial project was given an added edge of danger by the addition of human blood to the printing of the cover card.

said we wanted to silk-screen in human blood? They went insane for seven months, because no doctor would guarantee that you couldn't get AIDS from it. But they were very courageous about it—we found doctors who said that if you irradiated the blood it would be OK. The printer mixed ink with the blood so it would adhere. Mixing ink and blood was also a way of using graphic design to underscore Jenny's message about women, rape, and violence.

"Collaborating with Maira, she would write the text and start to sketch, and I would sketch type over her pencil drawings (often working with Emily Oberman). We'd go back and forth, and she'd have to cut copy or I'd say, this type could go here and it'd be nice if this character could raise their arms so we could tuck the type in their armpit. It was a completely integrated process, and there was a lot of trust. We would not use the computer until the production stage because we develop an idea and then use whatever production tool is most appropriate. Maira's first book was based on a song written by David Byrne, 'Stay Up Late,' and it was Byrne's name which helped get it published. After that Maira was able to do all these other projects that were much further out."

Maira Kalman continues, "I started writing books about ten years ago. I was painting before then but Tibor had the idea that I should collaborate on a book with David Byrne. People in our age group were just beginning to have kids—we'd had a really belated adolescence right into our thirties. I wanted to create books that were interesting for both adults and children. Books that were eccentric and full of humor and showed the world as I saw it: a kind of divine madness."

NOTORIOUS: HERB RITTS
Photography monograph, 1993

For this showcase of work by the acclaimed American photographer Herb Ritts, Kalman kept his design interventions to a minimum. By pairing images and cropping into the cover picture he lets the photographer's famed celebrity and fashion shots speak for themselves.

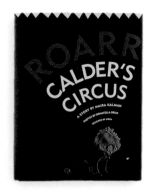

Taken from one of a series of children's books written by Maira Kalman, this cover and spread show how the husband-and-wife team collaborate. Typography is used creatively to emphasize meaning and thereby intensify the pleasure of reading.

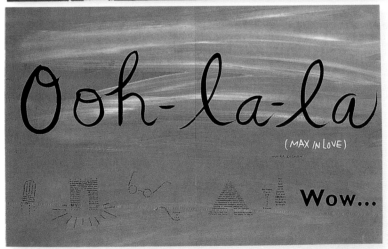

MAX MAKES
A MILLION,
OOH-LA-LA
(MAX IN LOVE)
Children's books,
1990, 1991

The mixing of Maira Kalman's hand-painted words with M&Co's typeset text adds another expressionistic device to the team's typographic palette.

23

M&CO DESIGNED identities and literature for a range of corporate clients. These included banks, real estate developers, and retail chains.

"With Red Square and The Limited, M&Co were giving the 'hipness treatment' to probably our most left-wing and right-wing clients. The Limited is a $6 billion retail empire which owns six chains of boutiques in malls all over the U.S. They're more decorative and feminine than, say, The Gap. They're trying to be hip, and wanted us to do an annual report. So we sold them hip perfume. Funnily enough, we did the same thing with Red Square.

"There was a guy constructing a very bland apartment building, and he wanted to give it a far-out image. He was a left-wing client in terms of the visual presentation he wanted. We're talking about the Lower East Side—the building is at Houston and Avenue B, which is a pretty nasty neighborhood. Real estate is interesting because it's just space. It has absolutely no identity, so you can create any kind of look for it. Image can often determine whether or not a real estate project succeeds. Here, the only thing that was predetermined was this very fucked-up neighborhood. We thought that only someone a bit strange (and with a fair bit of money) would want to live here. So we wanted to give the graphics an edgy identity, an aggressive name and this confrontational posturing. And the further Danny Abelson and I went, the more the developer loved our work."

ORCHESTRA
Logo for Knoll, 1990

For this corporate client M&Co came up with the name, concept, and logo. "Orchestra" is a furniture system developed by Knoll; the musical analogy conveys the idea of different but related elements working in harmony.

ORCHESTRA UNIVERSAL SYSTEM ACCESSORIES BY BRUCE HANNAH AND AYSE BIRSEL

RED SQUARE
Real estate brochure, 1989

Creating an identity for an urban development in a less-than-desirable area called for a design *tour-de-force*. This brochure employs so many clever folds and devices that a prospective buyer could not fail to be intrigued, or to aspire to its classy yet cool images of radical chic.

THIS IS ABOUT A YEAR IN THE LIFE OF A COMPANY.
THE STORY IS TOLD IN PICTURES AND WORDS AND NUMBERS.
THE MOST IMPORTANT CHARACTER IS NEVER SEEN. THOUGH
SHE IS CENTRAL TO THE STORY. SHE IS THE
CUSTOMER. THEREFORE SHE DO NOT APPEAR IN THE
NARRATIVE BUT EVERYWHERE.
THEY ARE THE ABOUT IS THE
SPIRIT OF THE COMPANY REPRODUCED
IN PICTURES OR WORDS OR NUMBERS, BUT WHICH IS SHARED
BY 43,000 PEOPLE WORKING TOGETHER. THIS IS THE STORY OF
THE LIMITED IN 1986.

THE LIMITED
Annual report, 1987

A giant U.S. clothing chain presents an unconventional image to its shareholders and industry peers. The device of printing the text over an "unsuspecting" image, in a blatant and almost confrontational manner, adds a touch of attitude to a corporate endeavor.

25

"M&CO GOT INVOLVED with Talking Heads totally by accident, through my partner Carol Bokuniewicz's network of party buddies. We were asked if we'd pitch to design the Brian Eno and David Byrne project, 'My Life in the Bush of Ghosts.' We said, we were born for this project. We pitched, they hated us, they went elsewhere. But when Brian was in the bathroom I kept saying to David, oh don't you need help with your record covers? We would be happy to do stuff on spec, and eventually David said, OK.

"It turned out they were sick of working on their covers. 'Fear of Music' had just come out and the blind-embossed cover had taken the band seven months of work. They were totally frustrated with the record company. For 'Remain in Light' we pitched two billion ideas, all of them materials-oriented—foam rubber, sandpaper, you name it. Mistakenly, we thought that was what they wanted. Then one day Chris Frantz and Tina Weymouth turned up with four pictures of their faces covered with red cursor masks, which had been produced at the MIT Media Lab, and it was a matter of arguing for two months about whether it should be like this, or like this. Then I sketched the words 'Talking Heads' with upside-down 'As' and the words run together, on a tiny piece of tracing paper, and just pinned it to the wall and forgot about it. But during a meeting I showed it to Chris and Tina who said, 'that's cool,' and the next thing I know it's graffiti on the streets of New York. You just have to rely on your sub-conscious and let your hand draw.

"We changed the Talking Heads type for every release, making it work with the title of the record. For 'Speaking in Tongues' we mis-set the type, forming nonsense words simply by making mistakes in the location of word spaces, because we were trying to make it look like another language. For 'Crosseyed and Painless' we made the cover look like a scientific equip-ment label, using blue and gray, and a boring

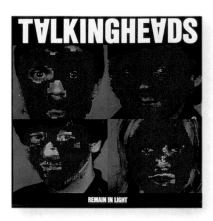

REMAIN IN LIGHT
Album cover, lyric sheet, and logo, 1980

Helping to turn an interesting pop band into a cult phenomenon, Kalman's artwork for Talking Heads built into a striking identity through constant reinvention. The band's sophisticated fans could interpret such a stance as an indication of aesthetic confidence. Kalman also used the lyric sheets (opposite right) **for subtle and early experimentation with expressionistic typography.**

3 BIG SONGS
EP cover, 1981

Members of Talking Heads also released solo efforts and collaborated with different artists on independent projects. Such occasions gave Kalman the opportunity to work with familiar clients but without the need to foreground the band's logo. Here, four simple icons, drawn by Maira Kalman, represent David Byrne and his songs.

TALKINGHEADS

THE GREAT CURVE   CROSSEYED AND PAINLESS   BORN UNDER PUNCHES (THE HEAT GOES ON)   HOUSES IN MOTION
ONCE IN A LIFETIME   LISTENING WIND   SEEN AND NOT SEEN   THE OVERLOAD

Take a look at these hands. They're passing in-between us.
Take a look at these hands.
Take a look at these hands. You don't have to mention it.
No thanks. I'm a Government Man.

And the heat goes on… And the heat goes on… And the heat goes on…
…goes on… Where the hand has been… And the heat goes on… And the heat goes on… And the heat
And the heat goes on… And the heat goes on… And the heat goes on… And the heat goes on…
…Where the hand has been… And the heat goes on… And the heat goes on…

I'm not a drowning man!
And I'm not a burning building! (I'm a tumbler!)
Drowning cannot hurt a man!
Fire cannot hurt a man. (Not the Government Man.)

All I want is to breathe   Thank you. Thank you
Won't you breathe with me?
Find a little space… So we move in-between   I'm so thin
And keep one step ahead of yourself.   I'm catching up with myself

All I want is to breathe
Won't you breathe with me   Hands of a Government Man
Find a little space so we move in-between
And keep one step ahead of yourself.   Don't you miss it! Don't you miss it!

And the heat goes on… And the heat goes on… And the heat goes on… And the
heat goes on… Where the hand has been… And the heat
goes on… And the heat goes on… And the heat goes on… And the heat goes on…
Where the hand has been… And the heat goes on… And the heat goes on… And the heat goes on…

TALKING HEADS

PRO-A-903

CROSSEYED AND PAINLESS

12 INCH SINGLE

STEREO   45 R.P.M.

CROSSEYED AND
PAINLESS
12" single cover, 1980

The cover imitates a scientific
equipment label; the illustration
is a medical device for cleaning
tubes.

DAVID BYRNE	3 BIG SONGS
45 RPM	BIG BUSINESS
MY BIG HANDS	BIG BLUE PLYMOUTH

photo from a scientific supplies house. The number featured on the front cover is the actual catalog number of the single.

"I think one of the most interesting things we did, and that was totally of the moment, was the lyric sheet for 'Remain in Light.' I did it completely by myself because it was just a type speccing job. I didn't know how to do mechanicals (artwork) at all, but I was good at speccing type to fit and look interesting. I listened to the songs endlessly and got the feeling of how the type could create narrative through the setting. The technology was wax and paste-ups. You order the type from a typesetter and two days later you get it back, and it's a mess, so you cut it all up again and have it reset. Then you're out of money, because they charge you each time, and it's a nightmare because you have very little control. It was an incredibly tense process because of the money involved. Talking Heads had no money, and we adjusted it two or three times. Each time you think, just a little bit more and it'll be perfect!

"Every music design we did was by accident. I never liked working with big acts, because I think their egos are really out of control. We did a Ramones record cover and they were the biggest lunatics I ever met in my life. Early on we did a Rolling Stones cover (for Europe) which was hideous because we were in awe of Mick and listened to him. Anytime we got to work with big stars we would turn out junk. Laurie Anderson and Talking Heads we could deal with because they were sane and very intelligent.

"David Byrne started a record label for international music, called Luaka Bop. 'O Samba' was the first release, a Brazilian compilation he put together. The thing I like most about that album is the back cover. That image isn't trying to fulfill any ideas, it's just a great picture because the photographer saw something incredible at a particular moment. You can't commission that."

SPEAKING IN TONGUES
Album cover detail, 1983

With the simplest of means the title and logo are transformed into an unknown, unpronounceable language (opposite).

THE NAME OF THIS BAND IS TALKING HEADS
Album cover, inner sleeve, 1982

"For this album we used every picture we had," recalls Kalman. The cover features snapshots of the band performing at a birthday party in their earliest days. Top left: front cover; top right: back cover; bottom: inner sleeve.

NAKED
Album cover, inner sleeve, 1988

The "Naked" album shows Kalman's ability to source eye-catching photographs. Featured here is the world's largest pickle, on tour at Times Square (opposite).

29

INCLUDES ESSAYS BY DAVID BYRNE AND CHARLES PERRONE

Samba & pagode

UM

1.
A DEUSA DOS ORIXÁS:
CLARA NUNES

2.
IJEXÁ (FILHOS DE GANDHY):
CLARA NUNES

3.
S.P.C.:
ZECA PAGODINHO

4.
SUFOCO:
ALCIONE

5.
FORMOSA:
CIRO MONTEIRO

6.
OLERÊ CAMARÁ:
ALCIONE

7.
O ENCANTO DO GANTOIS:
BETH CARVALHO

DOIS

1.
ALDEIA DE OKARIMBÉ:
NEGUINHO DA BEIJA FLOR

2.
QUEM ME GUIA:
ALMIR GUINETO

3.
ELA NÃO GOSTA DE MIM:
AGEPÊ

4.
CLAUSTROFOBIA:
MARTINHO DA VILA

5.
BATUCA NO CHÃO:
MARTINHO DA VILA

6.
SARAU PARA RADAMES
PAULINHO DA VIOLA

DESIGN: M&CO.
FRONT COVER PHOTO:
FROM URBAN BUSHWOMEN DANTE CO.
BACK COVER PHOTO:
H. ARMSTRONG ROBERTS, INC.
PHOTO STRIPS
FRONT COVER: C. MEYER, BLACK STAR
BACK COVER: SEBASTIÃO SALGADO, MAGNUM PHOTOS INC.
LUAKA BOP/SIRE RECORDS COMPANY,
75 ROCKEFELLER PLAZA, NEW YORK, NY 10019-6908.
MARKETED BY WARNER BROS. RECORDS INC.,
A WARNER COMMUNICATIONS COMPANY Ⓒ.
Ⓒ 1989 SIRE RECORDS COMPANY AND LUAKA BOP INC.
℗ 1985 EMI-ODEON FONOGRÁFICA, LTDA.
℗ 1986 COMERCIAL FONOGRÁFICA RGE LTDA.
℗ 1965, 1978, 1980 POLYGRAM DO BRASIL LTDA.
℗ 1976, 1985 BMG ARIOLA DISCOS LTDA.
℗ 1986 DISCOS CBS BRASIL
℗ 1984 CONTINENTAL GRAVAÇÕES ELÉTRICAS S.A.
THIS COMPILATION ℗ 1989 SIRE RECORDS
COMPANY. MADE IN U.S.A. ALL RIGHTS RESERVED.
UNAUTHORIZED DUPLICATION IS A
VIOLATION OF APPLICABLE LAWS.
™ IS A PROPRIETARY TRADEMARK OF LUAKA BOP INC.
ALL RIGHTS RESERVED.

LUAKA
BOP

30

LOST IN THE STARS: THE MUSIC OF KURT WEILL
Album cover, 1989

Overlaid onto a portrait of the celebrated writer are M&Co's trademark icons, one for each track. Look closely and you can see Restaurant Florent's typical steak representing the gravel-throated singer Tom Waits.

O SAMBA
Album cover, 1989

The front and back covers of this compilation album *(below and opposite)* **use photography to stunning effect. The typographic device of shadowing the figure from a stock shot (back cover) adds a dynamic sense of movement.**

DEFUNKT
Album cover, 1982

For this eponymous release by Defunkt, Kalman used a minuscule photographic detail, overlaid with challenging type in leisure-suit colors. At the time retro looks were being reinterpreted in both the fashion and music scenes, and Defunkt was one of the bands who so accurately supplied the soundtrack to such innovations.

WITH KALMAN'S self-confessed "short attention span" it is hardly surprising that he has experimented with a range of media. Tackling advertising, promotional videos, and film titles, Kalman views screen graphics as a route to movie-making that bypasses mainstream Hollywood.

"When you design titles it's between you and the director. In the early 1980s we did our first real titles, for a film about Trisha Brown, the dancer. It made us about four cents, but we stayed involved with Jonathan Demme's production company. Then with *Something Wild* it was just our turn. We don't do all his titles, but we did that and *Silence of the Lambs*.

"We would wait until the late production stage, when things were pretty much figured out, and see what mood he wanted to evoke. Then we'd make suggestions and try to engage him with those. With *Something Wild* we proposed corroded, eaten-up type, with the colors and drop-shadows biting each other. You often need drop-shadows on film titles, and we hate them, so the idea was to make them work as a design element, as opposed to it looking like art deco. We'd done a bunch of titles by this time. For my very first titles job I'd put the handwritten titles on the floor, used M&Ms as dividers between the titles, and the director panned it with a hand-held 8mm camera.

"What we're trying to do is make the motion more important than the type, and yet be disciplined enough to keep to the mood that the director wants the audience to be in as the

SOMETHING WILD
Feature film titles, 1986

For Jonathan Demme's film about a man being kidnapped from normality on a hot summer's day, M&Co used colorful, wobbly type that pulsates to the rhythm of the soundtrack. The end credits feature the mesmerizing singer Sister Carol, who keeps the audience from leaving the movie theater.

(NOTHING BUT)
FLOWERS
Promo video for Talking Heads, 1988

In this groundbreaking example of promo video making, Kalman animated Byrne's lyrics to create the narrative. The effect shown at right was created by projecting 16mm scrolling lyrics onto Byrne's face as he sang them.

TRUE STORIES
Feature film titles and
poster concept, 1987

The end titles for David
Byrne's feature film debut
featured a long shot
overlaid with type scrolling
at various speeds, recalling
an aerial view of cars on a
highway. The unpublished
poster concept treats the
film's content as stories in a
mock tabloid newspaper.

film opens. It's very important to set a mood in film titles. Some directors have the courage to do that, some don't. Jonathan makes so many different kinds of movies, and obviously he has to set things up very differently for *Silence of the Lambs* than for *Something Wild*.

"The ultimate example of us using titles as a way of getting involved in filmmaking is probably the Talking Heads video *(Nothing but) Flowers*, because that's a film designed around the witty interaction between performers and type. We used the same process as the Talking Heads lyric sheets [of marrying the narrative to the type]. It was made using dinosaur technology: we projected the lyrics onto David's face using a 16mm projector, and also supered words over the live action using a Harry editing machine—the latest thing in 1989 but now an antique."

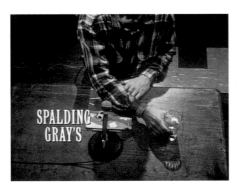

SWIMMING TO CAMBODIA
Feature film titles, 1988

While the live action footage was being filmed, Spalding Gray picked up his glass and put it down on the other side of the microphone. Kalman simply filled each empty space with type.

STICKY FINGERS
Feature film titles, 1987

In another attention-grabbing end-title sequence, the customary scroll of credits "plays-up" until it finally slips sideways from the screen.

TV and advertising

M&CO HAVE WORKED with a number of U.S. advertising agencies and created screen graphics and identities for niche-marketed television channels.

"We've done a bunch of promotional stuff for ad agencies. For Chiat Day we mailed out a brick to their clients—most of them were pretty annoyed. Chiat Day have the image of a young, arrogant, punky kind of agency. Jay Chiat is a visionary, and he commissioned us to design a presentation video. We made three video discs, to be run in sync, with the type moving from one monitor to another. It was a totally 'out there' presentation, and Jay was happy, but none of the account handlers would use it because they would just say to clients, 'we're here to do whatever you like!'

"We worked on a spot for Pepe Jeans, with Weiden and Kennedy, right from the ideas stage. We wanted to overload the screen, filling it with more ideas than we had space for. There are two ways to do that, one is double exposure, the other is split screen. We fell in love with different bits of imagery and decided they looked better all together rather than in sequence. We had a wonderful, very open relationship with that agency and the art director Michael Prieve. Also the Pepe account was very small in America at the time; we didn't have much money to spend and so everyone stayed away from us. As with everything else, the smaller the budget the more freedom there is, the bigger the budget the more people are frightened.

"The MTV project was different. It was meant to be entertaining information, just to show for instance how much pizza gets eaten per day in the U.S. (the answer is 75 acres). Again, we wanted to create an overload of information because that's how information is now. It wasn't an ident, it was a 15-second filler, a little bookend, which we shot as a 'practical' set-up. What you see on screen was in front of the camera—those objects were all shot on film, not composed electronically."

PEPE JEANS
TV ad, 1990

Kalman recalls how his team wanted to show more images than they had either the time or the space for. The solution was to use a split-screen device, and the resulting "screen within a screen" gives the appearance of an animated fashion spread.

CHIAT DAY
Promotional laser disc set, 1990

Kalman used some of his most challenging anti-narrative devices in this presentation, including mis-matched subtitles and a Hungarian commentary.

PIZZA SPOT
MTV broadcast, 1991

This tongue-in-cheek "information" spot was filmed live, but the end result resembles a strictly choreographed, computerized animation.

35

Christmas and self-promotion

"THE CHRISTMAS PRESENTS were about self-promotion and becoming our own clients. That was the one project a year when we could work for ourselves. The intention was to throw our creative weight around, get new work, send something to people we had no business talking to.

"With 'A Book of Words' we wanted to send out a dictionary but make it our own, so we thought we'd steal it in a very public way. We took a Merriam Webster standard college dictionary, ripped off the paper cover and had it rebound into a hardback using our own cover and endpapers. Our favorite part of dictionaries is the pictures, so we decided to recaption them. Sean Kelly, a writer friend, came up with the captions, and we put the recaptioned pictures on the endpapers. So a diagram indicating the parts of a chicken would be captioned 'McNuggets.' Everything would be askew, and on the cover it says, 'A Book of Words from M&Co as told to Merriam Webster.'

"We did a Christmas present that didn't have a name. Everyone got a different book. They were all 59 cents from the Strand, a big old secondhand bookstore. The idea was to give people cash—it was a conscience bomb. We made a horizontal pad which slotted into the back of the old book and acted as a series of bookmarks with copy. There were two voices throughout the text. It opened with 'Just a cruddy old book, is that all I'm getting?' And the copy in 'our' voice would list all the cruddy ideas we'd thought of giving. Then you turn a page and there's a dollar bill. And a voice says, 'what can I do with that?' Then $5, 'that's better,' and $20, 'now we're talking.'

"With $26 you could buy a meal. Then the next page said, 'or you could give it away.' And there follows three envelopes with stamps, one addressed to the Coalition for the Homeless, another to Gay Men's Health Crisis U.S., and one for the National Fund for Reducing the

M&CO COOKIES
Christmas gift, 1981

M&Co flaunted the real function of corporate gift-giving—to impress prospective clients. The early gifts were unadulterated acts of self-promotion, albeit with a playful slant, but as the company matured the gifts became more challenging.

M&CO RULERS
Christmas gift, 1983

A useful gift tinged with a few playful bits of nonsense, these wood and metal rulers—one for friends, another for clients—proved so popular that M&Co reissued them as products.

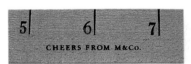

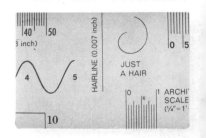

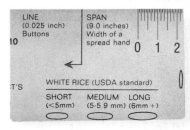

M&CO CHOCOLATES
Christmas gift, 1980

Guaranteed to prompt discussion in the recipient's

A BOOK OF WORDS FROM M&CO
Christmas gift, 1986

This appropriated dictionary must have looked very impressive landing on the door mat. Implying that M&Co had annexed the English language for its own misuse, this gift gave Kalman the opportunity to debunk the most staid publishing format. An overtly traditional binding is undermined on the endpapers by the absurdist recaptioning of previously innocuous dictionary illustrations.

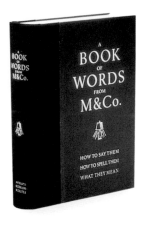

Deficit. You could send the money to any, or none, and no one would ever know. The next year we sent out a lunch of a peanut butter and jelly sandwich, an apple, a can of juice and a piece of poundcake with a note saying, 'that's the menu which is distributed to homeless people at Grand Central Station.' Underneath it all was a $20 bill and an envelope addressed to the Coalition for the Homeless.

"The other reason we wanted to do Christmas gifts was that we knew someday we could turn them into products. We tried for six months to make a rubber ruler you could stretch so that you could say, 'see it's nine inches, just like I told you.' But unfortunately we could not get it made.

"One year I went totally wild, and Maira was very encouraging, saying, 'just do it from the gut.' We had a bar of soap made that said TRUTH, and you were supposed to wash your hands with this to come clean. It was in a metal case that said 'Basta nostalgia'—'enough nostalgia' in Italian. It came with a little bottle of perfume called 'Optimism.'

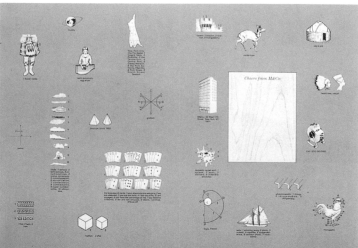

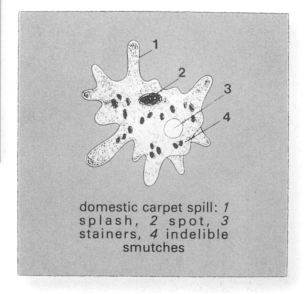

domestic carpet spill: *1* splash, *2* spot, *3* stainers, *4* indelible smutches

"In the last year of M&Co we sent out the Red Cross Box. There was a letter in it explaining why it couldn't be used as a first aid kit. This was because we'd asked our patent lawyer if there was a trademark owned by the Red Cross, and they said, sure, and there's an even bigger one owned by Johnson & Johnson, the pharmaceutical company. But the lawyer said, don't worry, they're my friends, I'll call them up and everything will be cool. The reply came, we're gonna sue their arses, especially if they associate it with first aid products. So that's why we sent it with a letter inside saying, 'please, this is not a first aid box.' The lawyers were just doing their lawyer thing. Apparently in the U.S. you have to send an incredibly stern letter as a warning. That's all you do, put them on notice, and that protects your trademark. Originally the gift was just a nice shaped box, but it became an exercise in ownership. And functionally, it's a good object. You can hang it on the wall, put stuff in it—but not Band Aids, OK?"

$26 CASH FOR CHRISTMAS
Christmas gift, 1990

A secondhand book contains a "conscience bomb" in the form of a printed conversation, a (real) dollar bill, a $5 bill, a $20 bill, and a choice of charity envelopes to ease the act of parting with the money.

RED CROSS BOX
Christmas gift, 1992

With the red cross box Kalman flouted trademark regulations while adopting a conciliatory stance—he included a letter requesting that it *not* be used as a first aid kit.

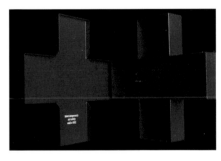

HOMELESS LUNCH
Christmas gift, 1991

People more used to expense-account dining were sent lunch boxes identical to those donated to New York's homeless at Grand Central Station. The box included $20 which they could donate to a homeless charity.

M&Co PRODUCTS EVOLVED from the company's Christmas gifts—an opportunity for them to be their own clients, to design in 3D, to promote themselves, and potentially to make products. This was a way of taking their ideas directly to the public.

"The paper weight of yellow ruled paper became the first M&Co product. It was a very good metaphor for what designers make because that was the type of paper we used in the studio. To us this is such an important object in that it reflects the way we think about things. It's the rejected idea that helps to make the good idea, it's the fuel. And we thought if we couldn't send out the crumpled paper, why couldn't we make this garbage permanent? It took a year to perfect the *trompe l'œil* prototype. It's made of rigid vinyl, screen-printed and heated so it's pliable, and hand-crumpled around some heavy metal. After Christmas we took the paper weights to what was then New York's only design store, Sointu, and they said, 'yeah we'll sell them.' We eventually did a blueprint version for architects, one with ledger paper for accountants, and another using stock market listings.

"We designed the watches for ourselves, which is the best way to design anything. Everyone in the studio came up with ideas. I'd look at

PIE
Watch, 1987

This watch design crams several dials onto the face, but leaves the wearer guessing for 75 percent of the time.

TEN ONE 4
Watch, 1984

Stretching the wearer's ability to read between the lines/numbers, this watch found its way into the permanent design collection at New York's Museum of Modern Art.

PAPER WEIGHT
Desk accessory, 1984

M&Co's witty series of paper weights, produced in screen-printed vinyl around a metal core, parodied the crumpled paper of rejected ideas.

ASKEW
Watch, 1984

This design *(above)* tests whether we can distinguish between misinformation and the obvious truth.

STRAPHANGER
Watch, 1987

Designed to be read at an angle of 90 degrees, this is a watch that can be shared with curious subway users. It can also be set to read conventionally.

Kalman's playfulness can be subtle. The reverse of this watch warns the wearer, "Waste not a moment."

41

these watches and think, there's no way in the world I wouldn't buy one if I saw it. And there are loads of designs because our salespeople wanted new stuff every year. My favorites are Ten One 4, which began as a sketch by Maira in among a million hats, trees, and cacti she was drawing; Askew, where the numbers are mixed up; Bang, where the numbers are too big; Pie, where only one-quarter of the face has any numbers; Straphanger, for reading on the subway; and Solo, with just one hand. Like lots of our work, the watches were a bit of a pain really.

"We made a product called Mystery based on the old idea of a book hollowed out for a gun. We did a whole series of these products which looked like books but turn out to be other things. The first we did was a stationery set, but then we did really wacky ones. The Fortune box was like an omen or a token, with a rabbit's foot and a four-leafed clover. The Romance volume, for Valentine's day, had a feather and a condom—it was all white and really beautiful.

"What's amazing is that these products continue to sell as well now, ten years after they were designed, as they did then. And I still get my employee discount."

FUZZY
Wall-clock, 1991

The fuzzy type treatment was achieved using a photocopier, before the handy blur option appeared on software programs.

BADGES OF
DISTINCTION
Enamel pins, 1992

A classy alternative to the standard lapel button, these meaningful but discreet adornments declare the wearer to be allied to Kalman's principles.

42

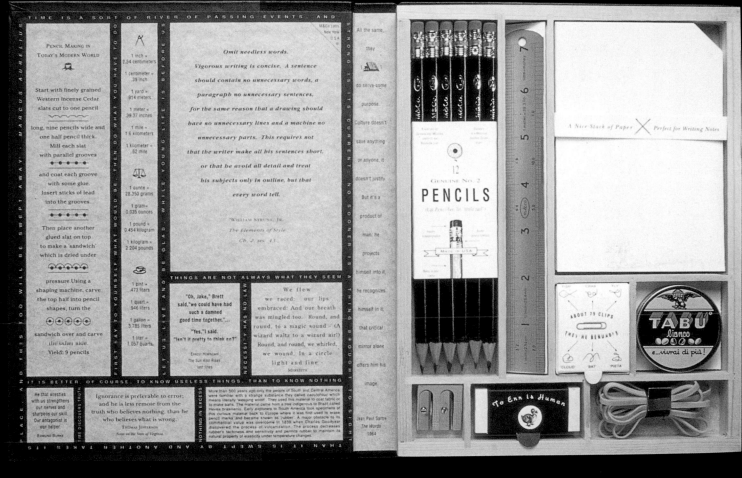

A MYSTERY
Stationery set, 1991

Clad in a book-shaped box, only the legitimate user can identify the M&Co product when disguised on a shelf. The set contains thoughtful quotes and all sorts of useful objects.

GLOBAL ALPHABET BLOCKS
Educational toy, 1992

Six of the world's alphabets— Arabic, Cyrillic, Roman, Hebrew, Latin, and Japanese—are given equal billing on these wooden building blocks, for word play by children and linguists alike.

43

KALMAN HAS WORKED with curators and planning authorities to create environments ranging from exhibition spaces to whole city blocks. He has been instrumental in designing the planning guidelines for the redevelopment of New York's 42nd Street.

"Redevelopment plans for Times Square and 42nd Street had been going on for 25 years, then in 1991 the State of New York decided to clean up the area. It was full of porn shops, junk food stalls, and low-life retailing, and it was a big drugs market. From 7th Avenue, past Broadway to 8th, was a very dangerous strip—so the State condemned those blocks on 42nd Street and moved everyone out.

"There had been plans to build giant towers, on four or five sites, but when the real estate market collapsed the developers stalled. They'd have gone bankrupt if they had built, but they were obliged to do something. So the State said, 'you give us 20 million dollars to fix up the street level and we'll give you seven years before you have to build.' Our fear as designers and planners was that the developers would want to turn the neighborhood into a place full of barren plazas and faceless office blocks—the sort now *de rigeur* on 6th Avenue. But they took our point of view,

and we had the opportunity to impose guidelines on the use and design of the area. These guidelines recognized that people had an affection for 42nd Street and they wanted to avoid the mindless fountains and 'keep off' signs.

"The State invited a group of designers to pitch ideas. We were asked to be on the Robert Stern team. I laid out a vision for the street, that it should be democratic, urban, exciting, and diverse—financially, economically, racially, and in every other way—that this is New York and it ought to be a great street. I argued that we had to cure the street, that it was sick, and that we could create a vibrant contemporary version of the street. What makes cities special is the cacophony, excitement, and democracy of the sidewalk, where everyone has equal access. That interaction is what gives cities their great energy. I was seeing 42nd Street not as a horrible nightmare, but as everybody's memory-vision from all the famous songs, plays, and movies.

"What had made 42nd Street exciting was the lights, the signs, and the ads, and its mixture of stores, theaters, and cinemas. That became our mantra. The idea was very simple and obvious, and cheap; we figured that we could sell advertising spaces, bring in more entertainment and

42ND STREET
"Everybody" billboard and design proposals, 1993

Drawings of "blue-sky" proposals were used to set out design guidelines, while public art such as the "Everybody" project reassured the public that progress was being made.

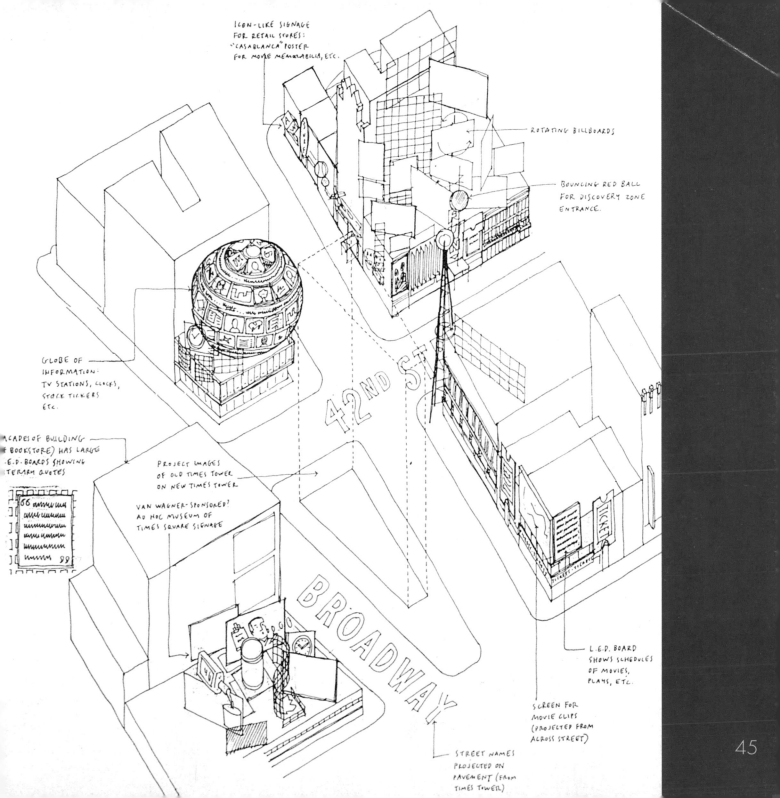

ICON-LIKE SIGNAGE
FOR RETAIL STORES:
"CASABLANCA" POSTER
FOR MOVIE MEMORABILIA, ETC.

ROTATING BILLBOARDS

BOUNCING RED BALL
FOR DISCOVERY ZONE
ENTRANCE.

GLOBE OF
INFORMATION:
TV STATIONS, CLOCKS,
STOCK TICKERS
ETC.

42ND ST.

...CADES OF BUILDING
(* BOOKSTORE) HAS LARGE
...E.D. BOARDS SHOWING
...TERARY QUOTES

PROJECT IMAGES
OF OLD TIMES TOWER
ON NEW TIMES TOWER

VAN WAGNER-SPONSORED?
AD HOC MUSEUM OF
TIMES SQUARE SIGNAGE

BROADWAY

L.E.D. BOARD
SHOWS SCHEDULES
OF MOVIES,
PLAYS, ETC.

SCREEN FOR
MOVIE CLIPS
(PROJECTED FROM
ACROSS STREET)

STREET NAMES
PROJECTED ON
PAVEMENT (FROM
TIMES TOWER)

45

NEW YORK: CITY OF AMBITION
Exhibition design,
Whitney Museum
of American Art, 1996

A bold use of typography,
color, and symbolic objects
characterized the displays
in these galleries.
The environment had to
contextualize a broad
range of artistic styles and
schools, and tell the
complex story of art in
New York from 1900 to
1960. Kalman co-curated
the exhibition with
Elizabeth Sussmann.

make it safe and clean and a tourist spot, all by 'un-designing' the area.

"We spent a year trying out and designing buildings and features—Scott Stowell made important contributions to this—none of which would be built. We designed a basketball court, almost all in glass, jutting out over the street. We dreamt up a vertical billboard park, which would have old and interesting advertising from all over the world, which you could climb through. That was all blue sky, but through it we developed the idea of how to turn a building into a sign. Once the visual concept was accepted, we spent another year writing design regulations and standards for the private developers.

"When we had finished that stage—coming up with the design motif—there was a year when nothing happened, when the project was up for review, specification, and budgeting. But we wanted to show something was going on and that was when we came up with the idea of an art show, using the street as a canvas. About 20 different artists did projects, and M&Co did the 'Everybody' billboard. It was painted yellow with this giant word symbolizing what 42nd Street is for. In order to make it participatory and fun, we suspended chairs on the lower part of the billboard, which went down to ground level. You could sit on them but they were just a little too high so your toes

would dangle and you'd feel like a little kid. You had to trust that the chairs would hold. Bums sat in the chairs, so did rich people, celebrities, and tourists—'everybody' meant just that. It stayed up for about a year.

"The great irony is that it was Disney who understood the vision. When they bought a theater on 42nd Street that kick started the whole area. Now rent is being collected and it's a miracle that this slum has become hot property in the New York real estate market. (Much credit should go to Rebecca Robertson, of the urban development corporation, for keeping the spirit of 42nd Street alive for so many years.) The development is far from perfect—everything is too new, and needs the dignity of age to feel right—but at least the street is alive and misbehaving again.

"*City of Ambition* was a show at the Whitney featuring art made in New York from 1900 to 1960. The installation was incredibly aggressive colorwise, with each decade shown in a totally different kind of gallery with a different kind of hanging style. We put type on the walls, had trees in the space, and designed one gallery that was completely black. *Strange Attractors: Signs of Chaos*, at the New Museum in New York, was another installation we designed. Here we pasted cheap Xeroxes all over the walls, and the art was hung right on top of it. We also designed the exhibition catalog" [see page 18].

STRANGE ATTRACTORS:
SIGNS OF CHAOS
Exhibition installation, New Museum, 1989

Kalman turned gallery walls into a chaotic landscape, using layers of Xeroxes to reflect the information overload and harsh realities of the world outside. His reasoning was that powerful art will be heard above the clamor.

47

KALMAN'S ROLE within the magazines he has been involved with has extended from controlling the look to being responsible for the entire content. Each new title has meant a step forward. Every new attempt, he promises, will be with the goal of radically changing how magazines work. "The field is moribund," he says.

"I art directed *Artforum* for about a dozen issues. Our layouts interacted with the art because we were trying to make the reader see something in the work which they might never have noticed without the type prompt.

"In 1989 I became creative director of *Interview*. Fabien Baron had just produced two brilliant issues but was fired, and I took over in an emergency and worked on it for two years. I would go to *Interview* every morning and then to M&Co in the afternoons.

"I didn't redesign the magazine. I used the typefaces Fabien Baron had picked because he had incredible taste, and he had set up a beautiful grid. All I did was enlarge the body copy, which was tortuously small. I don't think the issue is what typeface you use, it's what you do with it, how well you make it read. One is essentially stylistic and the other is about content, and you have to put this much content [big gesture] with this much style [tiny gesture]. Redesigns are fine, but really great ideas are what you need.

"*Artforum* and *Interview* had the same editor, Ingrid Sischy. I was a little frustrated by the fact that someone else was making the final decisions, but she was a really great editor, and I learned more from her than just about anyone else. She taught me how to look at pictures and photographs, which was something I really had not understood before. I would really beat up, crop, or misuse photographs, but she taught me to stay silent long enough to let a photograph talk to me. She showed me how to look for a

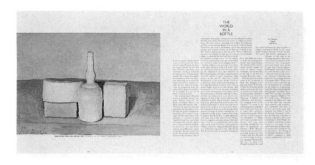

ARTFORUM
Spread, September 1987
Spread, December 1987
Cover, November 1987

Rejecting the conventions of magazine design, and the grids which restrict a designer to orderly but repetitive layouts, M&Co structured the text to echo the composition of featured artworks. Cover treatments were bold and playful. This film still, taken from *Bombay Talkie* made in 1970, reveals that both humor and kitsch are to be found in the early output of directorial duo Merchant Ivory. Kalman doesn't miss a trick positioning the magazine's logo.

ARTFORUM

NOVEMBER 1987 $6.50 I N T E R N A T I O N A L

49

very long time before making a decision, and to trust my instincts when I chose an image.

"*Interview* could have been a great magazine if it had concentrated on the notion of the extreme personality. I believe you have to be a maniac in order to change the way things are - think Napoleon, Helmut Lang, Frank Lloyd Wright, and Francis Bacon. The notion of the extreme personality was Andy Warhol's original idea when he started the magazine [in 1970]. That, together with the most boring, the most banal conversations.

"When I started *Colors* I got insanely busy. So I appointed an art director at *Interview*, Richard Pandiscio, and gradually left it up to him. He did an amazing job there."

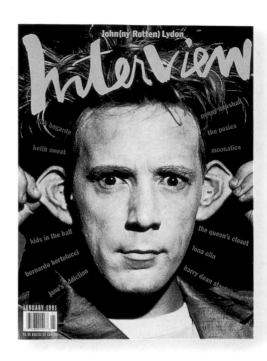

INTERVIEW
Covers (from left),
November 1991, June 1991,
September 1990

Kalman's cover treatments for *Interview* used typography to enhance the meaning of the cover photos—and sometimes to comment on a certain actress's self-absorption.

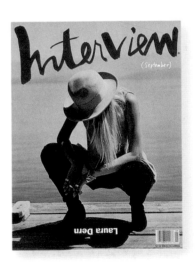

INTERVIEW
Cover and spreads,
January, 1991

Adding a spiky halo of type to the cover portrait *(opposite)* **reminds the reader of John Lydon's former incarnation as punk's pre-eminent icon, Johnny Rotten. Kalman learned to give good photography the space it deserves. This spread speaks for itself.**

INTERVIEW
Spreads (clockwise from top left), March 1991, August 1990, February 1991, October 1990

Opening spreads of magazine interviews usually comprise headline, credits, introduction, and pull-quotes, as well as the ubiquitous portrait and columns of text. Kalman jettisoned those conventions, preferring to fix on a device that underlined a particular characteristic of the subject—whether through the use of a crop, a color, heavy irony, or expressive typography.

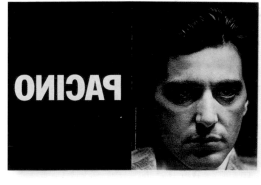

COLORS WAS AN INTERNATIONALLY distributed magazine sponsored by the Italian clothing company Benetton. Kalman was contacted by Oliviero Toscani, the creative director of Benetton, and asked to be the editor-in-chief. With the support of Toscani and Luciano Benetton (who owns the family-controlled business), both adopting a hands-off approach, Kalman was able to create a completely new concept in youth-oriented publishing.

"Benetton's concept was to found a magazine that would be international and targeted at a young audience. I agreed with these priorities and thought that the magazine needed to be primarily visual, since reading is now an endangered pastime. I believed it necessary to figure out a way to tell a story with pictures—to invert the usual relationship between words and images. And since it was a magazine aimed at young people all over the world, it had to be as relevant to a teenager in Manila as to one in Berlin or Cape Town.

"I must admit, it wasn't a magazine with a lot of 'voices'—it was mostly my voice. It may not have been a magazine at all, in terms of a collection of separate sections and features. It was more of a manifesto, which is not an unreasonable thing for a magazine to be when it starts because most have too many voices and are too compromised. Had I worked on it for longer (I did thirteen issues) it might have gained more voices, but I was so unsure of what I was doing that I was dictatorial about it. In any case I'd read that Condé Nast and Alexey Brodovich and Diane Vreeland had all been totally mad, you couldn't talk to them, and I think that's what you have to be like to start a magazine. You should listen to no one.

"A typical issue would begin with the inception of a theme; then I would sit in my room for a day or two and figure out what I wanted to know about that theme and madly dash off a

COLORS
Covers, 1991-95

These thirteen covers— produced during Kalman's tenure at _Colors_—show the range of topics covered. The aim was to be both universal and particular. Issues 1-3, unthemed; issue 4, Race; issue 5, The Street; issue 6, Oops! Ecology; issue 7, Fuck AIDS; issue 8, Religion; issue 9, Shopping; issue 10, Sport; issue 11, Travel; issue 12, Heaven; issue 13, Wordless.

COLORS

las tribus en nueva york
cowboys en polonia
el rey de tonga y la reina del ajo
(Y UN PRÍNCIPE O DOS)
desayuno en el tibet
(EN EGIPTO EN RUSIA Y EN LA COSTA DE MARFIL)
héroes en guatemala
(EN AFRICA DEL SUR Y EN TAILANDIA)
besos en todas partes

tribes in new york
cowboys in poland
breakfast in tibet
(AND EGYPT AND RUSSIA AND COTE D'IVOIRE)
king of tonga & queen of garlic
(AND A PRINCE OR TWO)
heroes in guatemala
(AND SOUTH AFRICA AND THAILAND)
kisses everywhere

C O L O R S
Cover, issue 1, autumn/winter
1991

Even though the first issue was not themed, it set the magazine's unconventional tone. The cover, appropriately enough, featured a new-born baby.

storyboard for each article. Sometimes I would use a word, and sometimes there would be a 'cloud-shaped' drawing of 'something' (that was a big joke with everyone). Then I would present the storyboards to the staff and have them challenge them, saying what they thought was boring or missing. There were text and photo researchers, who would have about five weeks to work on four stories each. And they would create the nuttiest telephone bills in history.

"We asked stupid questions. We'd call people in Finland and ask them what's on a slice of pizza and how much it costs. We asked people in Nigeria what was slang for condoms. (It's *okpuanu*, meaning 'penis hat.') Knowing that tells you more about a country than *Time* magazine can ever tell you. I think those little things add up to a realistic image of a place. I like to describe *Colors* as a magazine about the ways in which people are alike and the ways in which they're different, and we wanted the magazine to be on the intersection of those two ideas. So we only did articles about things that could be relevant everywhere—like snacks, garbage, or haircuts. It's what I like to call 'contemporary anthropology,' that quality of life on the planet in the present.

"Some people would say they weren't real articles, but we just wanted to keep people's interest. Since the information in the main part of the magazine was so lightning quick, we also wanted to create a three-dimensional bibliography at the back of each issue. We called this the 'Yellow Pages,' and put in it all the information we couldn't fit in the spreads. The Yellow Pages offered an opportunity for people to get involved, to contribute money, to volunteer, to get in touch, to buy a book, a CD, or a T-shirt, to make a live, realtime connection to the material they had just read.

"*Colors* was about its subject, not about its design. It was about having an idea and taking

COLORS
Yellow Pages spread

Taking its stylistic cue from the world-famous telephone directory, the Yellow Pages (below) **contained information on organizations to contact, books to read, and ways to take direct action.**

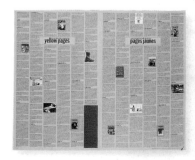

Kalman jettisoned the familiar sections of news, features, and reviews that generally lead a reader through a magazine. Instead he used the density of the layout as a way of varying the reader's pace. On the informative spreads, imagery was used with an almost scientific precision, while headline-grabbing photographs (such as the computer-manipulated celebrities, opposite) were presented in the form of an unmediated portfolio.

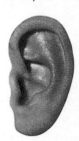

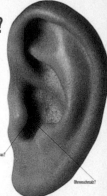

We have a lot in common: two ears, two eyes, a silly nose and roughly twenty square feet (and seven pounds) of skin...

SO, what's the **difference?**

Wir haben viel gemeinsam: zwei Ohren, zwei Augen, eine alberne Nase und etwa zwei Quadratmeter (drei Kilogramm) Haut...

also, was ist der **unterschied?**

brown skin?
braune haut?

black skin?
schwarze haut?

white skin?
weiße haut?

orange skin?
orange haut?

very white skin?
sehr weiße haut?

asian skin?
asiatische haut?

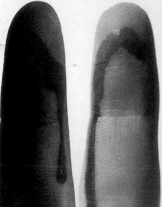

So, what's the **difference?**

Entonces ¿cuál es la **diferencia?**

noses?

eyes?

craniums?

¿narices?

¿ojos?

¿cráneos?

blood?

¿sangre?

and hair?

¿y el pelo?

nothing
nada

everything else away. When we made the cover of the *Daily Express* (featuring a computer-manipulated image of Queen Elizabeth as a black woman, from the Race issue), I thought we'd succeeded. We tried to venture where few magazines had gone. I loved to see how the media raised the issue of race, so did Oliviero and Luciano. They enjoyed the scandal and being the 'bad boys.' I'm very proud of that image.

"What I was after in the 'What if...?' story in the Race issue [number 4] was this. In order to figure out how much of a racist you are, take a person you already know and change their race. Try to feel how your reaction to them changes. When you saw Arnold Schwarzenegger as a black man, I was hoping you'd think, how is he different, is he stronger? If you look at the black queen, are you're thinking, would that queen have better music or style? If you do, then that's resorting to stereotypes, which is what racism's really all about.

"With the AIDS issue we were trying to figure out how we could create empathy for people with AIDS. We saw that the difference between people who cared about AIDS and people who didn't came down to whether or not they knew someone with AIDS. So we looked for a celebrity, someone that people would care about, to 'give' AIDS to. We chose Ronald Reagan because his face is well known and because he had a very negative position on AIDS. We wrote an ironic editorial, a parody of a loving obituary. It said that Reagan was the man who made the world aware of AIDS, made the schools give out information, and went onto a wartime footing with the manufacture of condoms. We said 'thank you' for saving 25 million people, and wasn't it a tragedy that he was the one to contract AIDS and was to die of it.

"That issue has the thickest press-cuttings book ever! But I think the Race and the AIDS issues really changed the people who saw them.

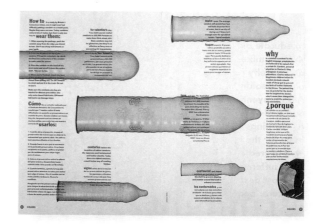

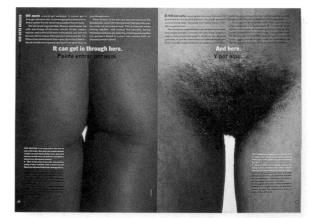

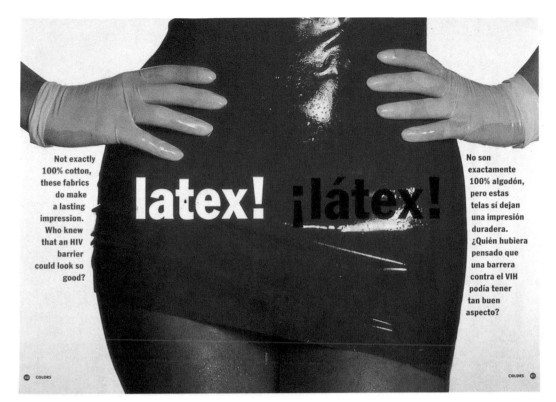

COLORS
Spreads, Fuck AIDS
(no. 7), fall 1994

In an issue that attempted to educate and empower, Kalman mixed fetish wear and novelty condoms with plain-speaking text about AIDS prevention. Statistics and real-life stories stand as warnings and provide hope for the future. The aim was to create empathy for AIDS sufferers and to dispel the most destructive barrier to a cure: apathy.

Not exactly 100% cotton, these fabrics do make a lasting impression. Who knew that an HIV barrier could look so good?

latex! ¡látex!

No son exactamente 100% algodón, pero estas telas sí dejan una impresión duradera. ¿Quién hubiera pensado que una barrera contra el VIH podía tener tan buen aspecto?

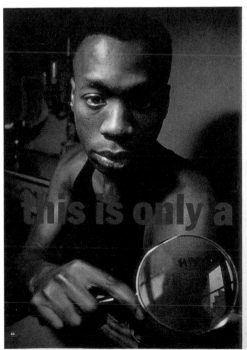

◄ Joseph Hawkins, 30, architecture student. "I was living with someone in 1981 who had been around a lot. About two years later, I was watching a TV special on AIDS and there he was, telling the world that he had AIDS! I think I screamed the loudest I have ever screamed, and obviously my first reaction was panic. The following week I went to a free clinic. When the test came back that I didn't have it, I still freaked out. I felt they had to be wrong. Now I do the test once a year."

◄ Joseph Hawkins, 30 años, estudiante de arquitectura. "En el 1981 viví con un hombre que había tenido muchas experiencias. Unos 2 años más tarde estaba viendo un programa especial sobre el SIDA en la tele, y ahí estaba él, ¡contándole al mundo que tenía el SIDA! Me puse a gritar, creo que nunca en mi vida había gritado tan fuerte, es obvio que mi primera reacción fue de pánico. La semana siguiente fui a una clínica. Cuando del análisis resultó que yo no tenía el VIH, yo seguía sintiéndome como loca, pensaba que se habían equivocado. Ahora me hago el test una vez al año".

You give some blood. You wait around.
You get an envelope.
These people know how it feels.
Te quitan un poquito de sangre.
Esperas un rato. Te dan un sobre.
Estas personas saben lo que se siente.

test
this is only a

esto no es más que un test

The AIDS test is actually a test for HIV antibodies. These are molecules produced by the immune system to attack foreign substances like virus or bacteria. When you get tested, a small amount of your blood is mixed with some chemicals. If HIV antibodies are present the mixture turns yellow.

If you're sexually active you should be tested every six months. It takes as long as six months for HIV antibodies to show up in the blood, so if you get tested just after you've been infected, your test could be negative even though there's HIV in your body.

El test del SIDA es en realidad un análisis para encontrar los anticuerpos contra el VIH. Se trata de moléculas producidas por el sistema inmunitario para atacar a substancias extrañas al organismo, como los virus y las bacterias. Cuando te hacen el análisis, mezclan una pequeña cantidad de tu sangre con algunas substancias químicas. Si los anticuerpos contra el VIH están presentes, la mezcla se pone de color amarillo. Si eres una persona sexualmente activa, deberías hacerte el test cada 6 meses. Pueden pasar hasta 6 meses antes de que los anticuerpos contra el VIH aparezcan en la sangre, así que si te haces el análisis inmediatamente después de haber sido infectado, podría resultar negativo aunque el VIH sí esté presente en tu organismo.

COLORS
Cover and spreads,
Wordless issue (no. 13),
September 1995

A whirlwind journey from
macro to micro, from the
stars to an atom, tells
the story of our planet
without the help of words.
A range of images—some
stunning, some shocking—
highlight the effect we
have on the environment,
and each other, and act
as a reminder that we are
not the sole owners of
Planet Earth. The idea
of letting images speak
for themselves was to
demonstrate that language
and cultural differences
need not be a barrier to a
shared understanding of
fundamental issues.

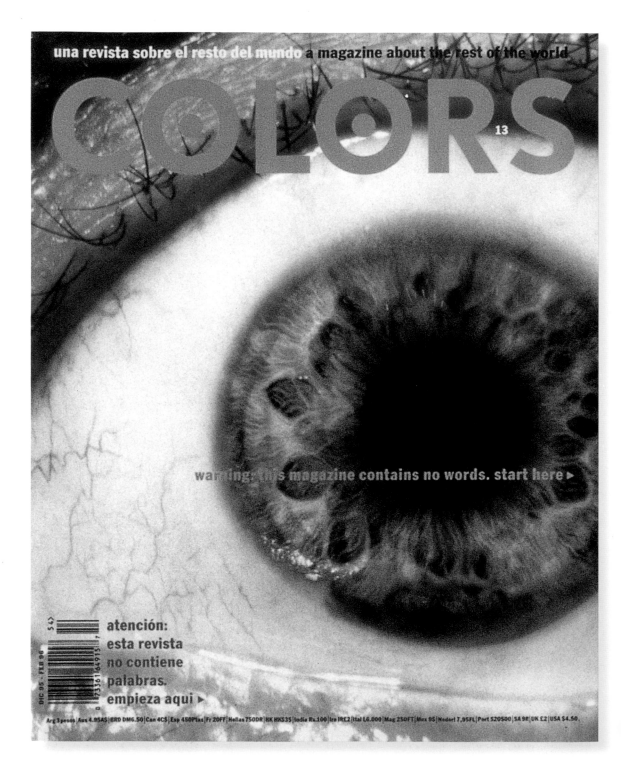

una revista sobre el resto del mundo a magazine about the rest of the world

COLORS 13

warning: this magazine contains no words. start here ▶

atención:
esta revista
no contiene
palabras.
empieza aqui ▶

DIC 95 - FEB 96

Arg 3 pesos | Aus 4.95A$ | BRD DM6.50 | Can 4C$ | Esp 450Ptas | Fr 20FF | Hellas 750DR | HK HK$35 | India Rs.100 | Ire IR£2 | Ital L6.000 | Mag 250FT | Mex 9$ | Nederl 7,95FL | Port 520$00 | SA 9R | UK £2 | USA $4.50.

"My last issue, sans words, was an experiment to see what would happen if we equalized things between readers and non-readers. (We weren't trying to suggest that different people read images in the same way—they don't.) That issue challenges the whole question of language. Design would have been yet another language, which we didn't need yet. Fernando Gutiérrez, the art director, did such a great job—it's very pretty and clean. You can choose pictures like a writer chooses words. We selected every image, examining about 25,000, one by one. Sizing was very important, and it was a painstaking process.

"We produced five issues of *Colors* in two-and-a-half years at M&Co in New York, and eight issues in two years in Rome. That was a wonderful place to live. The money, the families, the buildings, even the furniture are all hundreds of years old. It's a city where you do nothing, just live off family money and dabble in poetry, and everyone is just the same—it's a completely homogeneous society. I'd have liked to bring *Colors* to London or New York, or even Budapest, where I could actually speak to people. I left because Toscani wanted the magazine in Paris, and I very much needed the diversity of New York. I'd like to start another magazine."

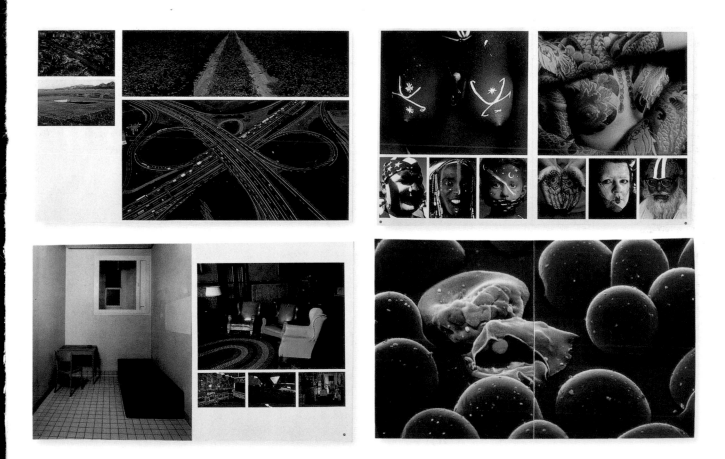

1949
Born in Budapest.

1956
Emigrates to U.S.A. with family.

1963-7
Attends Our Lady of Lourdes High School in Poughkeepsie, N.Y. (birthplace and headquarters of IBM). Works on school newspaper and yearbook. Interviews Timothy Leary for school paper after his lecture about LSD to IBM engineers.

1967-70
Attends New York University (NYU). Meets Maira. Studies journalism and history, and works on university newspaper covering the Columbia University student uprising. Joins SDS (Students for a Democratic Society).

1970
Drops out of NYU to cut sugarcane in the "Ten Million Ton Harvest" in Cuba. Loses weight.

1968-79
Works for company that eventually becomes Barnes & Noble (U.S. bookstore chain). Responsibilities include window displays, signs, store designs, ads, displays.

1979
Leaves Barnes & Noble to found M&Co. Company starts off "doing anything for money" but moves into cultural projects and toward creating content as well as form. Tibor and M&Co wander through all areas of design including graphics, film titles, TV spots, magazines, and architectural design. Clients include Manufacturers Hanover Bank, Formica, Talking Heads, Museum of Modern Art, Benetton, 42 Street Development Project, Hermann Miller, Knoll, The Limited, Subaru, Chiat Day, MTV, Vitra, WilliWear, and the Whitney Museum.

HERE'S YOUR
CLOCK
Cheers from M&Co.

1981
Marries Maira.

1982-5
Lulu Bodoni Kalman born. Alexander Tibor Dibi M.L. Onomatopoeia Kalman born.

1987-8
Art Director for *Artforum* (while running M&Co).

1989-91
Creative Director for *Interview* (while running M&Co).

1990
Recruited by Oliviero Toscani as founding editor-in-chief of *Colors*. Kalman works in New York on *Colors* from spring 1991 to fall 1993. Puts out five semi-annual issues.

1993
Toscani seeks full-time commitment to *Colors*; Kalman closes M&Co (at its peak) and moves with family to Rome. Magazine becomes quarterly; Kalman's team puts out eight more issues.

Fall 1995
Quits *Colors* and moves back to New York. Begins work as design consultant on a number of projects including redesign of lower Manhattan streetscape (for Alliance for Downtown New York); exhibition designs at the Whitney Museum; and communications and cultural projects for Barnes & Noble and Vitra International.

Index

Acknowledgments

Graphics

WILLIWEAR
Logo and press ad, 1988
Design: Tibor Kalman and Douglas Riccardi
Illustration: Douglas Riccardi

RESTAURANT FLORENT
Postcards, 1986
Design: Tibor Kalman, Alexander Isley and Dean Lubensky

Matchbooks, 1987
Design: Tibor Kalman and Alexander Isley

'Fuck Bush' press ad, 1988
Design and copywriting: Tibor Kalman

'Recycle' press ad, 1988
Design: Tibor Kalman and Tim Horn

CARBONELL
Press ad, 1988
Design: Tibor Kalman and Douglas Riccardi

AIGA HUMOR SHOW
Call for entries, 1986
Design: Tibor Kalman and Alexander Isley

ISAAC MIZRAHI
Press ad, 1991
Design: Tibor Kalman and Emily Oberman
Photography: Nick Wapplington

THE RIGHTS OF MAN
Poster, 1989
Design: Tibor Kalman and Douglas Riccardi
Photography: Chris Callis

Publications

STRANGE ATTRACTORS:
SIGNS OF CHAOS
Exhibition catalog, 1989
Design: Tibor Kalman and Marleen McCarthy

WORKSPIRIT
Catalog for Vitra, 1994
Design: Tibor Kalman

SUDDEUTSCHE ZEITUNG no. 46
Magazine spreads, collaboration with Jenny Holzer, 1993
Design: Tibor Kalman
Concept: Jenny Holzer
Photography: Alan Richardson

NOTORIOUS: HERB RITTS
Photography monograph, 1993
Design: Tibor Kalman and Emily Oberman
Publisher: Bullfinch Press

CALDER'S CIRCUS
Children's book, 1992
Text: Maira Kalman
Design: Tibor Kalman and Emily Oberman
Photography: Donatella Brun
Publisher: The Whitney Museum

OOH-LA-LA (MAX IN LOVE)
Children's book, 1991
Text: Maira Kalman
Design: Tibor Kalman and Scott Stowell
Publisher: Viking

MAX MAKES A MILLION
Children's book, 1990
Text: Maira Kalman
Design: Tibor Kalman and Dean Lubensky
Publisher: Viking

Corporate graphics

ORCHESTRA
Logo for Knoll, 1990
Design: Tibor Kalman and Dean Lubensky

THE LIMITED
Annual report, 1987
Design: Tibor Kalman and Alexander Brebner

RED SQUARE
Real estate brochure, 1989
Design: Tibor Kalman and Marleen McCarty
Photographer: Ken Schless

Music

REMAIN IN LIGHT
Album cover, lyric sheet, and logo, 1980
Design: Tibor Kalman and Carol Bokuniewicz
Record Label: Warner Bros

CROSSEYED AND PAINLESS
12" single cover, 1980
Design: Tibor Kalman
Record Label: Warner Bros

3 BIG SONGS
EP cover, 1981
Design: Tibor Kalman
Illustration: Maira Kalman
Record Label: Warner Bros

THE NAME OF THIS BAND
IS TALKING HEADS
Album cover and inner sleeve, 1982
Design: Tibor Kalman and Carol Bokuniewicz
Record Label: Warner Bros

SPEAKING IN TONGUES
Album cover detail, 1983
Design: Tibor Kalman and Bonnie Lutz
Illustration: David Byrne and Bonnie Lutz
Record Label: Warner Bros

NAKED
Album cover, inner sleeve, 1988
Design: Tibor Kalman and Douglas Riccardi
Record Label: Warner Bros

O SAMBA
Album cover, 1989
Design: Tibor Kalman and Emily Oberman
Photography: Chris Callis
Record Label: Luaka Bop

DEFUNKT
Album cover, 1982
Design: Larry Kazal and Tibor Kalman
Record Label: Select Records

LOST IN THE STARS:
THE MUSIC OF KURT WEILL
Album cover, 1989
Design: Tibor Kalman and Alexander Isley

Screen

SOMETHING WILD
Feature film titles, 1986
Design: Tibor Kalman and Alexander Isley
Directed by: Jonathan Demme
Production company: Religioso Primitiva

(NOTHING BUT) FLOWERS
Promo video for Talking Heads, 1988
Directed by: Tibor Kalman
Design: Tibor Kalman and Emily Oberman
Produced by: Joe Beirne

TRUE STORIES
Feature film titles and poster concept, 1987
Design: Tibor Kalman and Tim Horn
Directed by: David Byrne

SWIMMING TO CAMBODIA
Feature film titles, 1988
Design: Tibor Kalman and Douglas Riccardi
Directed by: Jonathan Demme

STICKY FINGERS
Feature film titles, 1987
Design: Tibor Kalman and Alexander Brebner
Directed by: Melanie Mayron

TV and advertising

PEPE JEANS
TV ad, 1990
Design: Tibor Kalman and Emily Oberman
Art Director: Michael Prieve
Agency: Weiden & Kennedy

CHIAT DAY
Agency credentials laser disc set, 1990
Content and design: Tibor Kalman
Directed by: Marc Chiat

PIZZA "INFORMATION" SPOT
MTV, 1991
Design: Tibor Kalman and Emily Oberman
Thumbs: Mike Mills

Christmas and self-promotion

M&CO COOKIES
Christmas gift, 1981
Design: Tibor Kalman and Carol Bokuniewicz
Baking: Sandy Green

M&CO CHOCOLATES
Christmas gift, 1980
Design: Tibor Kalman and Carol Bokuniewicz

M&CO RULERS
Christmas gift, 1983
Design: Tibor Kalman

A BOOK OF WORDS FROM
M&CO
Christmas gift, 1986
Design: Tibor Kalman and Alexander Isley
Copy: Sean Kelly

RED CROSS BOX
Christmas gift, 1992
Design: Tibor Kalman

$26 CASH FOR CHRISTMAS
Christmas gift, 1990
Design: Tibor Kalman and Dean Lubensky
Copy: Tibor Kalman

HOMELESS LUNCH
Christmas gift, 1991
Design: Tibor Kalman and Scott Stowell

Products

PAPER WEIGHT
Desk accessory, 1984
Design: Tibor Kalman

PIE
Watch, 1987
Design: Tibor Kalman and Alexander Brebner

TEN ONE 4
Watch, 1984
Design: Tibor Kalman and Maira Kalman

ASKEW
Watch, 1984
Design: Tibor Kalman and Alexander Isley

STRAPHANGER
Watch, 1987
Design: Tibor Kalman and Maid Marion McLusky

FUZZY
Wall-clock, 1991
Design: Tibor Kalman

BADGES OF DISTINCTION
Enamel pins, 1992
Design: M&Co

A MYSTERY
Stationery set, 1991
Design: Tibor Kalman and Douglas Riccardi

GLOBAL ALPHABET BLOCKS
Educational toy, 1992
Design: Tibor Kalman and Scott Stowell

Environment

42ND STREET
"Everybody" billboard, 1993
Design: Scott Stowell and Tibor Kalman

42ND STREET
Design proposals, 1993
Design: Tibor Kalman and Scott Stowell
Collaborating architects: Robert Stern and Paul Whelan

NEW YORK: CITY OF AMBITION
Exhibition design, Whitney Museum of American Art, 1996
Design: Tibor Kalman and Lana Hum

STRANGE ATTRACTORS:
SIGNS OF CHAOS
Exhibition installation, New Museum, 1989
Design: Tibor Kalman

Magazine design

ARTFORUM
Ice floes spread, September 1987
Design: Tibor Kalman and Emily Oberman

Georgio Morandi spread, December 198
Design: Emily Oberman and Tibor Kalm

"Bombay Talkie" cover, November 198
Design: Tibor Kalman

INTERVIEW
Covers and spreads
Design: Tibor Kalman and Richard Pandiscio

River Phoenix and Keanu Reeves cover, November 1991

Susan Sarandon cover, June 1991

Laura Dern cover, September 1990
(photography: Kurt Markus)

John Lydon cover and spread, January 1991 (photography: Kurt Marcus)

Lisa Minnelli spread, March 1991
(photography: Michel Haddi)

Joan Chen spread, August 1990
(photography: Wayne Maser)

Al Pacino spread, February 1991
(photography: Brigitte Lacombe)

Don King spread, October 1990
(photography: Michel Comte)

Colors

COLORS
Covers, 1991-95
Editor: Tibor Kalman
Design: Tibor Kalman (1-13) and Emily Oberman (issue 1), Gary Joepke (issue 2), Paul Ritter (issues 3, 4, and 5), Scott Stowell (issues 6, 7, and 8), Mark Porter (issues 9-12), Fernando Gutiérrez (issue 1)

Spreads, Race issue (no. 4), winter 199
Editor: Tibor Kalman
Design: Tibor Kalman and Paul Ritter

Yellow pages spread (no. 3), summer 199
Editor: Tibor Kalman
Design: Tibor Kalman and Gary Joepke

Spreads, Fuck AIDS (no. 7), fall 1994
Editor: Tibor Kalman
Design: Tibor Kalman and Scott Stowell
Photography: Sergio Merli (condoms), Oliviero Toscani (nudes, latex), Daniel Lainé (test)

Cover and spreads, Wordless issue (no. 13), September 1995
Editor: Tibor Kalman
Design: Tibor Kalman and Fernando Gutiérrez

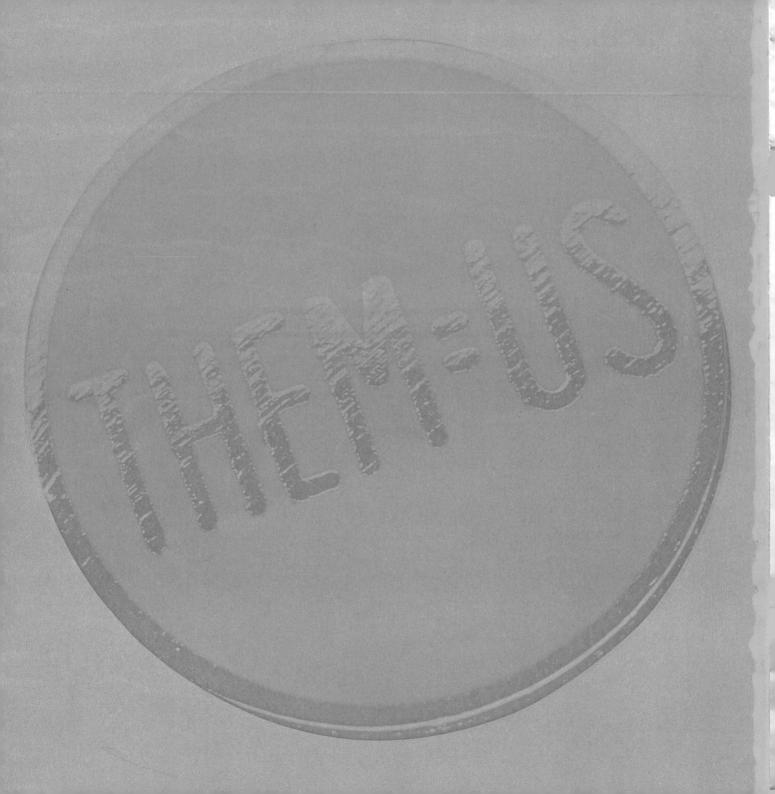

THEM:US

17. July.12 Midwest 33'2 85449